GET SMART ABOUT

WALT
DISNEY

Adam Kent

Get Smart about Walt Disney
by Adam Kent

Published by Rocket Books, Inc.
New York, NY, USA

For kids...
who dream big,
who work hard to become better,
who get up when they fall,
who know we are all human and
all worthy of respect and success.

For my son Little Adam...
who lights up my life.

May your dreams come true.

This book is for you.

ABOUT THIS BOOK

This biography book for kids is meant to be a fun, brief and educational exploration of an extraordinary person's life. Reading biographies is a great way to learn from extraordinary people who have experienced extraordinary things. While you read through the books in this series, think about the lessons you can learn from the stories and how they can help you figure out what to do and what not to do in your own life!

As you read this book you will find bolded words. You will find the definitions of the bolded words at the end of the page they first appear on. You will also find interesting facts listed at the end of each chapter about information that came up throughout the chapter.

I hope you enjoy learning about this extraordinary person!

Have a great time reading,

Adam Kent

CONTENTS

GET SMART ABOUT

WALT
DISNEY

Adam Kent

WALT DISNEY
AT A GLANCE

Walt Disney is one of the most recognizable names in the world. His creations provided fun and happiness to millions of children around the world for many decades. As co-founder of Walt Disney Productions he won 32 Academy Awards as of 2021 for a vast collection of inspiring animated films. Disney the company has won 135! He also created Mickey Mouse and founded the theme parks Disneyland and Walt Disney World. His legacy and creations will continue to provide joy for millions more for many years to come.

WALT DISNEY
FAST FACTS

1. Walt Disney was born in Chicago, Illinois in 1901.

2. Believe it or not, Walt Disney not only created Mickey Mouse, but he was also the voice of him!

3. During World War II, he created animated videos for war advertisements. These were in support of the U.S., and many made fun of the Nazi Party from Germany that committed some of history's most horrible crimes.

GET SMART ABOUT WALT DISNEY

CHAPTER 1

THE EARLY DAYS

Walt Disney was born on December 5, 1901. He was born in Chicago. He lived there for the first few years of his life. However, he and his family then moved to Missouri where he spent most of his childhood.

Walt Disney had a pretty large family growing up. In his household was his father, Elias Disney, and his mother, Flora. He also lived with four siblings, three brothers and a sister! His brothers were named Herbert, Raymond and Roy. His sister was named Ruth.

When Walt was four, the family moved to a town named Marceline in Missouri to live and work on a farm that his uncle Robert had recently purchased. There the family was religious and actively attended a local church.

It was in Marceline that Walt began developing a love of the arts with drawing and painting. He started drawing by copying cartoons from a section of a local newspaper that his mother subscribed to. He developed a skill with practice. He even started selling his artwork to family and neighbors as a boy! This hobby and skill is one that he put to good use later in his life.

In 1911, the family moved again, this time to a different city, Kansas City. You may guess that Kansas City is in Kansas, but it is in Missouri! This new city would introduce Walt to some important experiences that would shape the **trajectory** of his future.

The first experience that impacted Walt's future involved trains. Walt's uncle worked on a train as a train engineer. The line he worked on ran from Iowa to Missouri. It was while watching his

---

trajectory /trə-ˈjek-tə-rē/ noun: the path that an object or projectile follows through space <example: The trajectory of the rocket was carefully calculated.>

uncle work with trains that Walt became **fascinated** with them. During his youth he even started working on the train line, selling newspapers and snacks to the people riding the train. This experience helped shape Walt's lifelong love of trains, which later inspired him to include trains as a major **feature** in his theme parks.

The second experience that really helped shape Walt Disney's life happened as the result of a friend that he made in the new

---

fascinate /ˈfas-ə-ˌnāt/ verb: to interest or captivate someone greatly <example: The story of his life fascinated me.>

feature /ˈfē-chər/ noun: an aspect or quality that makes something notable or attractive <example: One of the features of the city is its beautiful parks.>

town. In elementary school, Walt made a friend named Walter Pfieffer. Walter's family became friends with Walt's whole family as well.

Walter's family had a strong interest in theatre at the time. They introduced the Disney family not just to theater, but also vaudeville and motion pictures. Vaudeville was a popular form of theatre in the 1890s through the early 1900s before motion pictures were made. It was a type of show that was light and funny, not **dramatic** like some other theater. At the time, motion pictures were also just starting to

---

dramatic /drə-'ma-tik/ adjective: relating to or involving an exciting or dramatic event or situation <example: The sudden change in the weather was dramatic.>

be made.

In Kansas City, Missouri, Walt also developed his drawing skills further. Walt went to school and also worked two newspaper routes with his brother before and after school during the week. However, he was so **ambitious** that even though he must have been very tired and needed to rest, he still took art classes at a local art institute to practice cartooning on Saturdays.

After grade school, Walt's father bought stock, which is a form of ownership of a company, in a jelly company and moved the

---

ambitious /æm-ˈbi-shəs/ adjective: having a strong desire to achieve something <example: She is an ambitious young woman who always strives for the best.>

family back to Chicago, just in time for high school. Walt went to a high school in Chicago called McKinley high school. There, he took drawing classes. He also got a job drawing cartoons for a local newspaper. This was a big accomplishment for a boy still in high school!

The cartoons that Walt drew were political cartoons. Walt was **patriotic** about being American. The cartoons showed this. A lot of the cartoons were about a war that was going on at the time, World War I.

Walt became so patriotic during the war that he was inspired

---

patriotic /pə-'trī-ə-tik/ adjective: relating to love for and devotion to one's country <example: He is a patriotic person who always supports his country.>

to quit school to join the army. He tried his best to join, even lying on the application about his birthdate! He was rejected, though, because he was too young.

After failing to join the army, Walt decided to join the Red Cross. The Red Cross is a **charitable** organization that helps people who have been hurt by war and other tragedies. He successfully joined in September of 1918. He was scheduled to help in France as an ambulance driver. He arrived in France in November. However, he arrived late. In mid-November the

---

charitable /ˈCHār-ə-tə-bəl/ adjective: relating to giving money or other forms of support to those in need <example: She is a charitable person who always donates to charity.>

land fighting of World War I ended. His help there was then no longer needed.

Walt was in France until 1919. During his time in France, he continued to draw cartoons. Some of his cartoons were even published in a newspaper called Stars and Stripes. After a short while, Walt headed back to America to start anew as an adult.

CHAPTER 1
FUN FACTS

1. Walt Disney was born in Chicago, Illinois, and spent most of his childhood in Missouri.

2. Walt's uncle got him first interested in trains. Trains became a major theme at Disney parks!

3. Walt's family was very interested in theatre. They were especially interested in early motion pictures. This interest helped inspire Walt's dreams and ultimately what Disney would become.

CHAPTER 2

FAMILY MATTERS

Walt Disney was born to parents named Elias Disney and Flora Call. Elias was an Irish immigrant from Canada, and Flora was from Ohio in the United States. They had a total of five children together, including Walt.

Elias Disney was both a construction worker and an

entrepreneur. He originally came to the United States with his father from Canada in search of gold in California in 1878. Later, his father bought land in Kansas, which they unsuccessfully tried to grow oranges on. Elias also worked other odd jobs, such as for a railroad company, as a professional fiddle player, and even as a substitute teacher, helping to fill in for his sister Anna in Kansas schools when she couldn't work.

It was working as a substitute teacher in Kansas where Walt's

---

entrepreneur /ˌän-trə-prə-ˈnər/ noun: a person who starts and runs a business <example: She is an entrepreneur who started her own company.>

father first met his mother. Flora Call, the woman who would become Elias's wife and mother of Walt Disney, worked as a teacher at the school where Elias substituted on occasion. Flora and Elias fell in love in Kansas.

At some point after Walt's parents started to date, Flora and her family moved to Florida. Elias didn't want to end the relationship, so he followed Flora to Florida. Walt Disney's parents married in 1888 in Florida.

Together Elias and Flora worked as managers of a hotel for a while in Daytona Florida. The hotel name was the Halifax Hotel. Elias worked as a mailman for a while as well. Later, they even bought some land in Kissimmee

Florida to try an orange farm there! It was not successful. But Kissimmee, Florida is very close to where one day his son Walt would establish Walt Disney World!

After their unsuccessful farming attempt in Florida, Elias moved with Flora to Chicago where he became a construction worker. That is a lot of jobs he had! Have you been counting? Though there were many jobs he had that he was unsuccessful at, his entrepreneurial spirit was powerful and clearly was passed down to Walt Disney!

As a construction worker in Chicago Elias worked at the World Columbian Exhibition. This Exhibition is rumored to have been an inspiration for Walt Disney's theme parks!

The World Columbian Exhibition was also known as the Chicago World's Fair. It was celebrated in 1893 to mark the 300-year anniversary of when Christopher Columbus landed in what would become the United States.

After working at the World's Fair, Elias continued with construction work and worked his way to becoming a building contractor. He bought and rebuilt homes in order to resell them. He also bought a small portion of a jelly company. Later, at the request of his brother, Elias moved the Disney family to Kansas to try farming again. Years later, after falling ill, he moved back to Chicago and continued construction work. He tried his hand at quite a lot of jobs!

Elias Disney as a father was strict. He wanted to teach his children about hard work and discipline. His children worked hard from a young age. He kept the money they made for "safe-keeping" because he didn't want them to waste it on unnecessary spending. He was also known to be a disciplinarian. When the kids misbehaved, he would discipline them with a stick. This was more **customary** in the past. Today this is not acceptable as a form of punishment as it was in the past.

---

customary /ˈkəstəˌmerē/ adjective: usual, habitual, or according to a custom or tradition it <example: our customary dinner celebration>

Walt Disney's mother, Flora, helped Elias with some jobs early in their marriage. However, for most of her adult life, she focused on maintaining her family and caring for her children. She brought her children up with a focus on religion. She also had a strong belief system and had to in order to make as many moves around the United States as being married to Elias Disney required her to!

Flora believed that the moves and all the job changes were all about making the family stronger and increasing their wealth, so she followed along with Elias's **ambitions**, while raising the kids.

---

ambition /æm-ˈbi-shən/ noun: a strong desire to achieve something <example: His ambition is to become a successful businessman.>

Flora was a loving and attentive mother. She made home cooked meals and sewed most of the clothes that the kids wore. She encouraged her kids to enjoy learning and to look forward to each new day.

After the kids grew up, Elias and Flora moved to Oregon where a couple of them lived. What happened next, though, was a real tragedy. In 1938, Wal and his brother had already made the film "Snow White and the Seven Dwarves." It was such a great success, that they surprised their parents with a home in Burbank, California near where they had their Disney production company.

Flora and Elias loved the home they were given. However,

Flora complained of a smell coming from the gas furnace in the house. She told Walt about the smell, and he sent workers from Disney productions twice to fix the furnace.

Sadly, a couple of days after Thanksgiving in 1938, and just a month or two after they had moved in, Flora went to sleep and never woke up. She died from breathing in the furnace fumes. It was a tragedy that Walt never stopped blaming himself for after. Elias also never fully recovered from the tragedy and loss of his wife and died a few years later.

Walt Disney had three brothers and one sister. They were named Herbert, Raymond, Roy and Ruth. Herbert grew up to have a successful career with the post office. Raymond owned an insurance company that insured the Walt Disney Company. Roy worked as a co-founder of the Walt Disney Company and led the company even after Walt Disney's death.

Lastly, Ruth was a talented organ player. She also was extraordinarily close to Walt. Walt wrote letters to her throughout his life whenever they were away from each other. These letters, which she eventually donated to the Walt Disney Hometown Museum in Missouri, are the best source of information about what happened with their company as it grew into the giant company it remains today.

CHAPTER 2
FUN FACTS

1. Walt Disney's father was an entrepreneur who tried many businesses.

2. Walt's father taught the importance of hard work, discipline and saving money.

3. Walt's mother died in a tragic accident from a gas leak in a house he had bought for his parents.

CHAPTER 3

A UNIQUE EDUCATION

Walt Disney was a person who made up for what he lacked in formal education with ambition and creativity. He actually never had a formal college education. He dropped out of high school as well in order to attempt to join the army.

Walt never did go back to school after whoever, as an adult he became so successful that he was eventually awarded honorary degrees from the **prestigious** universities of Harvard, Yale, the University of Southern California, and UCLA (The University of California at Los Angeles)! He was also a big **advocate** of continuing education in his later years.

One more interesting fact about Walt Disney's education is

---

advocate /ˈadvəkət/ noun: a person who supports or recommends a cause <example: She is an advocate for animal rights.> /ˈadvəˌkāt/ verb: to support or recommend a cause <example: He advocates for animal rights.>

prestigious /pre-ˈsti-jə-wəs/ adjective: respected and admired because of achievement, reputation, or social status <example: The university is one of the most prestigious in the country.>

that Walt was held back for two years before he was placed in school as a kid. The reason he was held back was because his sister was two years younger, and his parents wanted them to start school together. They thought that doing so would help them form a close bond that would keep them close throughout their lives. Indeed, it did!

CHAPTER 3
FUN FACTS

1. Walt Disney did not have a formal college education. However, because he became so successful, he was offered honorary degrees from colleges.

2. Walt Disney started school two years later than usual so that he could attend with his siblings.

CHAPTER 4

A CAREER TO REMEMBER

After serving in the American Red Cross in France just at the end of World War I, Walt returned to America and moved to Kansas City, Missouri, again. This time, he returned to begin his career.

Pesmen-Rubin Commercial Art Studio

In Kansas City, Walt first got a job at a local art studio named Pesmen-Rubin Commercial Art Studio. The year was 1919. He worked as an **apprentice** drawing **illustration** for printed advertisements and theater booklets. There, Walt met a man named Ub Iwerks who you will learn played an important role in the

---

apprentice /ə-ˈprən-təs/ noun: a person who works for and learns a trade from a skilled worker <example: He became an apprentice to a carpenter to learn the trade.>

illustrate /ˈi-lə-strāt/ verb: to show or demonstrate something using examples or diagrams <example: The teacher illustrated the concept with a diagram.>

development of Disney the company! After working at the art studio until just 1920, the business closed because they did not make enough money.

Walt and Ub decided to start a business of their own. This business did not last. At first, the two decided Walt should work somewhere else for a while to make money for it, while Ub tried to get customers and run the new business. However, they didn't get the customers they needed to stay open, so they closed the business as well. Ub went to work at the same place Disney had gone to. It was called Kansas City Film Ad Company.

After working at the new company for a while, Walt became

interested in what he thought was a new type of animation called cel animation. Walt started to experiment with the new type at home. The owner of the ad company he was working for was using a style called cut-out animation. Walt suggested the owner try the new kind of animation, but he didn't want to.

Laugh-O-Gram Studio

Since the owner of the ad company Walt was working for at the wasn't interested in trying the new animation called cel animation, Walt decided to start his own animation company. He asked a man named Fred Harman from the Kansas Film Ad Company to joining him, and later also asked Ub. One of their first clients was a company called the Newman Theater. Walt and his partners made short animations for the theater that they called *Laugh-O-Grams.* They were a hit!

The *Laugh-O-Grams* were partly inspired by Walt's love of *Aesop's' Fables* animation created by a cartoonist named Paul Terry. A fable is a story that is made up but teaches a lesson. Walt liked the idea of telling a story with a lesson. Walt's unique version were his *Laugh-O-Grams,* which were basically short fairy tales.

The *Laugh-O-Grams* for the Newman Theater were so successful that Walt was able to open his own studio. He called the studio Laugh-O-Gram Studio. He then hired animators, who were professionals who worked on making the animations.

Unfortunately, the studio was not able to make enough money to stay open, and after just a couple of years, they had to close the business. However, just before closing, Walt Disney had tried to make money by producing a 12-minute film of *Alice in Wonderland* that combined live acting and animation. This effort was worthwhile. It helped him find success later, as you will see!

Disney Brothers Studios

After having to close his studio, Walt decided to move to

Hollywood in Los Angeles, California. At the time, New York was the center of the United States for cartoons, but Walt had decided to try acting and film directing as a change of pace. He also had a brother, Roy already living there.

Walt wasn't successful at acting, but the move turned out to be a lucky one anyway. There weren't any cartoon studios in Hollywood animation studios during that time. Also, a film **distributor** named Margaret Winkler was looking for a new film series and knew about Walt's *Alice*

---

distributor /də-ˈstrə-byü-tər/ noun: a person or company that supplies goods to retailers <example: The distributor is responsible for getting the product to the customers.>

series. She reached out to Walt and offered him a contract to produce six films, much like those he produced at the Laugh-O-Gram studio in Missouri.

Walt accepted the offer and came up with the idea to start one the first animation studio in California. He realized that he would have an **advantage** being the first to do so, so he invited his brother Roy to help him open up an animation studio. Roy accepted.

Walt and Disney created the Disney Brothers Studio, the studio that would later become Walt Disney Studio. Fortunately, the

---

advantage /əd-ˈvan-tij/ noun: a favorable condition or circumstance <example: He has the advantage of experience over his competitors.>

studio was successful almost from the start because of the Alice contract. Walt even invited Ub to help make them.

After success with the Alice films, Margaret Winkler passed the film distribution responsibilities to her husband Charles Mintz. At the time, he was working with a company called Universal Pictures. He wanted new material, and asked Walt to come up with some.

Walt decided he wanted to try making an animated only film. The Alice and Wonderland films combined live acting and animation. Walt and Ub created a character they called Oswald the Lucky Rabbit. Oswald the Lucky Rabbit was well received.

Because of his new success, Walt decided to try to **negotiate** for more money. He traveled to New York to speak with Charles Mintz about the possibility. Charles pushed back and actually offered less money to Walt. By then, Mintz had also convinced most of Walt's animators to work with him. This put Walt in a bad position. Walt faced a hard decision: should he accept less money or should he part ways and lose his animators. Walt ultimately refused Mintz's ultimatum. He also learned then that Universal Pictures owned the rights to his Oswald the Lucky

---

negotiate /nə-'gō-shē-āt/ verb: to discuss and reach an agreement with someone <example: They negotiated a deal to buy the company.>

Rabbit character. When he declined to accept less money, He was basically forced to walk away and stop working with Mintz. It also meant he had to start over again, with a new character and new animators.

As luck would have it, while on a train back to California after the bad experience with Charles Mintz, Walt Disney came up with an idea that would change the world. In the midst of the anger, frustration and pressure of having to start over Walt came up with his most popular character of all time. Can you guess which character this was? It was Mickey Mouse!

Mickey Mouse

After coming up with the idea of Mickey Mouse on the train back to California from New York, Walt then had to sell it. Both Walt and Ub worked on the Mickey Mouse character. Ub took Walt's sketches and improved them. Walt developed the personality of Mickey Mouse and was his voice for the first couple of **decades**. A Disney employee once said, "Ub designed Mickey's physical appearance, but Walt gave him his soul."

One interesting fact about

---

decade /ˈde-kād/ noun: a period of ten years <example: The 1990s were a decade of great change.>

Mickey Mouse is that Walt first wanted to call him Mortimer Mouse. It is understood that Walt's wife told him that it sounded too **pompous**. She suggested the name Mickey instead.

In order to bring Mickey Mouse to life, Walt Disney needed money to pay animators to make films. Walt Disney approached many bankers to try to find **investors** for Mickey Mouse. Many bankers turned him down, a lot!

---

pompous /ˈpäm-pəs/ adjective: having or showing an exaggerated sense of one's own importance <example: He is a pompous person who thinks he is better than everyone else.>

investor /in-ˈves-tər/ noun: a person or entity that invests money in a venture with the expectation of making a profit <example: He is a successful investor who invests in real estate.>

How many would you guess turned Walt down before he found one to invest? Actually, it has been reported that around 300 bankers turned him down before one said "yes." This is remarkable and a true **testament** to the fact that for even the most successful people have seen many failures on their path.

After receiving money to pay for making Mickey Mouse cartoons, Walt and Ub completed two short animations called *Plane Crazy* and the *Galloping Gaucho.* They were unable to find distributors for either. Walt found a distributor for

---

testament /'te-stə-mənt/ noun: a statement or declaration that expresses one's beliefs or values <example: His life was a testament to his love of family and community.>

their third attempt at bringing Mickey Mouse to life. This short animation was called *Steamboat Willie*. The new distributor was Pat Powers from Universal Pictures.

With his success with Mickey Mouse, Walt started focusing on improving sound and animations in his films. He developed a successful series called *Silly Symphonies*. With these successes, he decided to approach Pat Powers to ask for more money for films. This is similar to what he had done in New York.

Unfortunately, Powers refused to give Walt more money. Even worse, Powers signed Ub to work for him instead of with Disney. This meant that Walt lost his long-time partner! It was a huge loss for

Walt. Walt lost another employee who thought that Ub leaving Disney would mean that it would close!

Soon after these losses, Walt Disney suffered what is called a "nervous breakdown." The emotions that he felt over the losses and from overworking for so long became so **overwhelming** that he had to stop working for a while to recover. To help him recover from the upsets, Walt and his wife Lilian spent some time vacationing in Cuba and Panama.

---

overwhelming /ˌō-vər-ˈhwel-miNG/ adjective: too great or intense for someone to handle or cope with <example: The amount of work was overwhelming, and he couldn't keep up.>

Academy Awards

After taking a break to recover, Walt started working again. Soon after, he signed a contract with a new distribution company called Columbia Pictures. With the help of Columbia Pictures, Mickey Mouse cartoons became more and more popular. Disney Studios created more popular characters like Goofy, Pluto and Donald Duck.

Walt Disney was ahead of the curve at using sound in cartoons. This means that he was one of the first. The same is true with color. In the early 1930s, Walt Disney started making color films.

One of his first color films was called *Flowers and Trees*. This film was well-received. It was so well received that it actually won an Academy Award In 1932 for Best Short Subject (Cartoon). At the very first Academy Awards ever. In case you do not know, the Academy Award is the highest award that you can win in the United States for Film and TV.

The next year, Walt Disney released the *Three Little Pigs* cartoon short. This won him his second Academy Award in 1933. This short was so successful that it has been called the most successful short cartoon "of all time!"

After winning the awards and starting to make all of his films in color, Walt Disney got another bright idea. He decided to make his first full length film. All of his previous films were short cartoons. His first full-length film was *Snow White and the Seven Dwarves*. This took four years to make. It also took a lot of money. It took so much money, that the newspapers at the time were guessing it would fail.

Walt Disney spent three times more than he wanted to spend making the moving. He wanted the film to be **groundbreaking**. He developed more **innovative** ideas.

---

groundbreaking /ˈground-ˈbrā-kiNG/ adjective: involving new and innovative ideas or methods <example: groundbreaking technology.>

innovative /i-ˈnä-və-tiv/ adjective: introducing new ideas or methods <example: The company is known for its innovative products.>

For example, in order for the animals in the movie to seem more realistic, he sent his animators to school and even brought in animals and actors so that they could study the movements and draw better for the film.

Snow White and the Seven Dwarves was a huge success. It even became the best-selling film up to that date. This time was so successful for Disney, that museums have called it the "Golden Age of Animation."

World War II

Soon after *Snow White*, Walt Disney made *Pinocchio*, *Fantasia*, and *Bambi*. Unfortunately, these films were not as successful. A war had started in Europe, so people were not going to the theaters as much. Still, the company suffered big losses and grew a big **debt.** Walt decided to help pay for some of his losses by making Disney a public company and offering stocks to the public. When the public buys stock in a company, they provide money to the company in exchange for ownership of a tiny piece of it.

Walt also cut the **salary** of his

---

debt /det/ noun: money that is owed to someone else <example: He is in debt due to excessive spending.>

salary /ˈsal-ə-rē/ noun: a fixed amount of money paid to an employee, typically on a monthly or annual basis <example: He negotiated a higher salary before accepting the job.>

animators and other employees at the same time. He felt this was a necessary move. However, the move really upset his employees. They went on strike for 5 weeks in 1941. Even though there was an agreement reached to help end the strike, the experience upset the employees so much that many quit Disney. Others who stayed continued to feel upset after.

The strike had interrupted the production of *Dumbo*, a film which earned some well-needed success and **acclaim**. Shortly after, though, United States entered World War II. For a short time, Walt made some

---

acclaim /ə-'klām/ noun: enthusiastic approval or praise <example: The play received widespread acclaim from critics.>

political films in response to the war. He formed the Walt Disney Training Films Unit to produce instruction films for the military. He also produced several **propaganda** films, including the Oscar-winning short film *Der Fuehrer's Face* and the feature film *Victory Through Air Power.*

However, these films did not generate enough revenue to cover costs, and Disney's studio was facing a debt of $4 million by 1944. Despite this, the Bank of America chairman saw the potential in Disney's work and gave him the

---

propaganda /prə-ˈpä-gən-də/ noun: information, ideas, or opinions that are spread to promote a particular cause or ideology <example: The government used propaganda to convince people to support the war.>

time he needed to market his product.

Post-War Success

Walt Disney's career after World War II was filled with many exciting and innovative projects. After the war, people were looking for ways to escape the hardships they had faced. Walt provided just that through his creative vision and storytelling abilities.

Walt slowly started to rebuild and recover from the financial losses. One way he accomplished this was to expand Disney into television. During this time, Walt produced new television shows called *The Mickey Mouse Club* and *Davey Crockett*.

In the late 1940s, Walt's production of short films decreased as competition from other animation studios like Warner Bros. and MGM increased. In response, Walt created a series of popular live-action nature films titled *True-Life Adventures*. *Seal Island* was the first film in the series. This film won yet another Academy Award for Best Short Subject.

In 1950, Walt released his first feature-length animated film, *Cinderella.* The film was a huge success. The film and the success of it showed that Walt was still at the top of his game when it came to animation.

The story of Cinderella was timeless. Its message of hope and

perseverance spoke to people of all ages. After *Cinderella*, Walt Disney continued to release hit after hit, with films like *Alice in Wonderland*, *Peter Pan* and *Lady and the Tramp*.

Disneyland

Walt Disney continued to innovate and bring new ideas to the entertainment industry. He was always looking for new ways to bring magic and joy to audiences around the world. One of his most significant contributions was the creation of Disneyland, the first-

---

perseverance /ˌpər-sə-'vir-əns/ noun: the quality of continuing to try to do something even when it is difficult <example: She demonstrated great perseverance in the face of adversity.>

ever theme park.

Disneyland was built on a 160-acre plot of land in Anaheim, California. Its doors opened to the public on July 17, 1955. Walt Disney wanted to create a clean and unspoiled place where children and families could go and have fun. He was inspired by the Tivoli Gardens in Copenhagen, Denmark. He made sure that Disneyland would be a combination of yesterday's pleasant memories and tomorrow's dreams.

The park was designed as a series of themed lands, linked by the central Main Street, U.S.A. which was a **replica** of the main

---

replica /ˈre-plə-kə/ noun: an exact copy or reproduction of something <example: The museum has a replica of the ancient statue.>

street in Walt's hometown of Marceline. The theme park offered something for everyone, including rides, family-friendly experiences, and meet-and-greets with Disney characters.

Disneyland was a huge success from the start, attracting 20,000 visitors a day after only a month of operation. By the end of its first year, the park had welcomed 3.6 million guests. Over the years, Disneyland continued to expand, adding new attractions and branching out globally with parks in Tokyo, Paris, Hong Kong, and Shanghai. The park was also home to the Disneyland Railroad, a train that linked all the themed areas and offered scenic tours around the park.

Walt's original vision for Disneyland was to create a magical world of adventure that would inspire and delight visitors of all ages. This vision has been carried forward to this day, and Disneyland continues to be one of the world's most popular tourist destinations. It is a place where memories are made, and the magic of Disney is alive and well.

Walt's Career After Disneyland

In the late 1950s, Walt Disney continued to push the boundaries of what was possible in animation and filmmaking. He released *Sleeping Beauty* in 1959, which was widely praised for its animation and timeless story. In the 1960s, he continued to innovate by introducing new television shows such as the *Disneyland* television show and the *Walt Disney's Wonderful World of Color* series. These shows allowed people to experience the magic of Disney from the comfort of their own homes.

Walt also started making live-action films in the 1960s. Some of the most popular films from this era include *Mary Poppins* and *The Sword in the Stone*. These films allowed Walt to showcase his **versatility** as a filmmaker and

---

versatility /vər-sə-ˈtī-lə-tē/ noun: the ability to adapt or work with many different things or in various ways <example: She is known for her versatility in playing different musical instruments.>

demonstrated his ability to tell great stories in a variety of ways.

Sadly, Walt Disney passed away in 1966. He had smoked for many years. He found out he had lung cancer and died after a short time. However, Walt Disney's **legacy** lived on through the company he had built.

Throughout his career, Walt Disney won a total of 22 Academy Awards. Can you believe it? This is more than any other person ever. He received 4 more honorary Academy Awards. He also received 4 Golden Globe Awards and 7 Emmy Awards.

---

legacy /ˈle-gə-sē/ noun: something that is handed down from an ancestor or predecessor <example: The company's legacy is a commitment to quality and customer satisfaction.>

Walt Disney was not only an animator but also a producer, director, screenwriter, voice actor, and theme park designer. He was a true visionary who revolutionized the animation industry and brought new technologies to the world of entertainment. Disney, the company, has continued to release new films, theme park attractions, and television shows since that have captured the hearts and imaginations of audiences around the world.

CHAPTER 4

FUN FACTS

1. When Walt Disney was just 18 years old, he moved to Kansas City to start his first animation studio, Laugh-O-Gram Studio.

2. Walt co-founded The Walt Disney Company in 1923.

3. Walt created one of the most iconic characters in the world, Mickey Mouse. Mickey Mouse appeared in the short film "Steamboat Willie" in 1928 and became a cultural phenomenon.

4. Walt Disney was not only an animator. He was also a producer, director, voice actor, screenwriter, and theme park designer. He was a true visionary who changed the animation industry and brought new technologies to the world of entertainment.

5. Walt Disney won 22 Academy Awards during his career, more than any other individual in history. He also won 7 Emmy Awards and 4Golden Globe Awards.

CHAPTER 5

HOBBIES AND PASSIONS

Walt Disney had hobbies that he enjoyed in his free time. One of his most prominent hobbies was art and drawing. From a young age, Walt showed a keen interest in drawing and storytelling. He even sold his drawings as a boy.

He also had a big love for trains. He had a personal fascination with trains and even has a miniature train in his office. He also built a small steam-powered railroad in his backyard called the "Carolwood Pacific Railroad." The train was ⅛ the size of a normal one and ran for half a mile.

Walt Disney was a visionary entrepreneur who not only revolutionized the entertainment industry but also made significant contributions to charitable causes. Throughout his life, he felt a strong passion to give back to the community and made donations to many different charities, clubs, groups, and organizations that he felt passionate about.

One of Walt's most notable contributions to the world of art and education was the creation of the California Institute of the Arts (CalArts). CalArts continues to be a leading art and design school today.

Walt's creative genius also shone in his idea to create an attraction for the 1964 World's Fair. The ride was called "It's a Small World," and its success provided an opportunity to raise funds for a noble cause. The proceeds from the ride were donated to UNICEF, the United Nations Children's Fund, to help save and improve children's lives around the world.

He provided financial support to organizations such as the Cerebral Palsy Foundation and the

March of Dimes, as well, which helped children with disabilities receive the care and resources they needed.

Walt Disney was also involved in environmental conservation and was a strong advocate for wildlife preservation. He was passionate about preserving the natural world for future generations and wanted to educate the public about the importance of conservation. He worked with organizations such as the National Wildlife Federation and the World Wildlife Fund to support their efforts in protecting the environment and wildlife.

Disney as a company continued Walt's charitable work and expanded it considerably. One of Disney's most notable charitable efforts is their work with the Make-A-Wish Foundation and other wish-giving organizations. Disney has granted more than 145,000 wishes globally, between Make-A-Wish and other wish-granting organizations, with an average of 11,000 wishes granted annually through 100 different wish-granting organizations. Wishes would range from trips to Disney theme parks and resorts, movie premieres, visits from favorite celebrities and characters, and much more.

Disney also supports a number of other charitable causes. Through programs like the Disney VoluntEARS program and the Disney Conservation Fund, the company has made a significant impact on the world, helping to improve the lives of children, protect the environment, and support the arts.

Disney has also made a commitment to empower youth through its Disney Future Storytellers program. This program includes programs that provide hands-on experience and inspiration to young people interested in careers in media, entertainment, technology, and hospitality.

Disney's support for STEM education is demonstrated through its partnership with FIRST, a robotics community that introduces youth to STEM through team-based robotics programs.

Their commitment to diversity is shown in their support for The

Hidden Genius Project, a non-profit that trains and mentors Black male youth in technology creation, entrepreneurship, and leadership skills.

In 2018, Disney committed $100 million to reimagine the patient experience in children's hospitals. As a result of this commitment, Disney introduced several programs, including Disney-themed Starlight Gowns, the Disney Movie Moments program, and a partnership with Starlight Children's Foundation to deliver toys, books, games, and other normalizing items to seriously ill children in the hospital. These initiatives have helped ease the anxiety of hospital stays for countless children and have brought moments of joy and comfort to children and their families.

Walt Disney's legacy extends far beyond the creation of Mickey Mouse and Disneyland. His philanthropic efforts have made a lasting impact on the world and continue to inspire future generations to give back to their communities and make a difference in the world.

CHAPTER 5
FUN FACTS

1. Disney has granted over 145,000 wishes for children through Make-A-Wish and also other wish-granting organizations.

2. He was a strong supporter of World War II and wanted to donate his studio services to the government for training purposes.

3. The proceeds from the ride "It's a Small World" were donated to UNICEF to help save and improve children's lives around the world.

4. The Walt Disney Company has continued Walt's philanthropic legacy and has supported a number of charitable causes, including granting wishes for children with Make-A-Wish, empowering youth through its Disney Future Storytellers program, and committing $100 million to improve the experience of children patients in children's hospitals.

CHAPTER 6

A PERSONAL LIFE

Walt Disney was a creative genius and a visionary who changed the entertainment industry forever. He was also a loving husband and father who valued family above all else. Walt met his wife, Lillian Bounds, in the late 1920s, when she was working as an ink artist at the Disney Studio. Despite a rough start to their relationship, with

Lillian initially rebuffing Walt's advances, the two soon fell in love and got married in 1925. Together, they built a strong and loving partnership that lasted for over 50 years.

Lillian was a supportive and caring wife who encouraged Walt in his **endeavors.** She played a significant role in the development of the Disney Studios, offering suggestions and constructive criticism. She also was content providing him with a comfortable home.

Walt and Lillian had two children, Diane and Sharon, who

---

endeavor /en-də-ˈvȯr/ noun: an attempt or effort to achieve a goal <example: It was a difficult endeavor, but they were determined to succeed.>

were born in the 1930s. Sharon was adopted. This was a fact that they did not hide. However, they also did not like it when the public mentioned it.

Despite being a busy and demanding man, Walt always made time for his family and was known to be a doting father. He often took his children on trips and adventures, and they were a constant source of inspiration for him.

Walt's love for his family was evident in the way he built his business empire. He wanted to create a place where families could come together and have fun, and he worked tirelessly to achieve this goal.

Despite the demands of his career, Walt never lost sight of the importance of family. He and Lillian remained deeply committed to each other throughout their lives, and his children were a constant source of joy and inspiration to him. He often spoke of his family as his greatest accomplishment, and his love for them was evident in all that he did.

CHAPTER 6

FUN FACTS

1. Walt Disney married Lillian Bounds in 1925 and they stayed married for over 50 years until Walt's death.

2. Walt and Lillian had two children, Diane and Sharon.

3. Walt and Lillian's daughter Sharon was adopted.

CHAPTER 7
A LASTING LEGACY

Walt Disney's legacy is a timeless gift to the world that continues to inspire across generations. Through his boundless creativity and innovative spirit, he brought to life a magical world that lives in our hearts and imaginations.

Walt's legacy is woven into the enchanting stories and characters he created, from Mickey Mouse to Cinderella, from Simba to Elsa. These characters teach us about courage, kindness, and the power of dreams. His legacy extends beyond entertainment, as he envisioned and built places like Disneyland, that bring joy to millions each year.

Perhaps the most profound part of Walt's legacy is his unwavering belief that dreams can come true. He transformed his own humble beginnings into a world where magic exists, reminding us all to chase our dreams with determination and creativity.

INSPIRATIONAL QUOTES

Quotes are like magical words that can lift your spirits and make you feel like you can conquer the world! They are short and powerful sentences that carry big messages. Quotes come from inspiring people who have experienced many things in life. They teach us valuable lessons, remind us to be brave, and encourage us to follow our dreams.

So, whenever you need some inspiration or a little boost of confidence, just read a quote, and you'll feel like you can achieve anything! Here are a few quotes from Walt Disney to inspire you on your way!

" If you can dream it, you can do it."

" The way to get started is to quit talking and begin doing."

" The more you like yourself, the less you are like anyone else, which makes you unique."

" Laughter is timeless, imagination has no age, and dreams are forever."

" It's kind of fun to do the impossible."

" The difference between winning and losing is most often not quitting."

" All our dreams can come true if we have the courage to pursue them."

" I only hope that we never lose sight of one thing—that it was all started by a mouse."

"   All the adversity I've had in my life, all my troubles and obstacles, have strengthened me... You may not realize it when it happens, but a kick in the teeth may be the best thing in the world for you."

"   The idea of waiting for something makes it more exciting."

BOOK
DISCUSSION

How do you think that Walt Disney's upbringing contributed to his success?

_____
_____
_____
_____
_____
_____

What challenges did Walt Disney face in his career, and how did he overcome them?

_____
_____
_____

_____
_____
_____

How did Walt Disney's passion for storytelling impact how movies and theme parks are made today?

_____
_____
_____
_____
_____
_____
_____

GLOSSARY

acclaim /ə-'klām/ noun: enthusiastic approval or praise <example: The play received widespread acclaim from critics.>

advantage /əd-'van-tij/ noun: a favorable condition or circumstance <example: He has the advantage of experience over his competitors.>

advocate /'advəkət/ noun: a person who supports or recommends a cause <example: She is an advocate for animal rights.> /'advə,kāt/ verb: to support or recommend a cause <example: He advocates for animal rights.>

ambition /æm-'bi-shən/ noun: a strong desire to achieve something <example: His ambition is to become a successful businessman.>

ambitious /æm-'bi-shəs/ adjective: having a strong desire to achieve something <example: She is an ambitious young woman who always strives for the best.>

appreciate /ə-'prē-shē-āt/ verb: to be grateful or thankful for something <example: I really appreciate your help.>

apprentice /ə-'prən-təs/ noun: a person who works for and learns a trade from a skilled worker

<example: He became an apprentice to a carpenter to learn the trade.>

charitable /'CHār-ə-tə-bəl/ adjective: relating to giving money or other forms of support to those in need <example: She is a charitable person who always donates to charity.>

customary /'kəstə,merē/ adjective: usual, habitual, or according to a custom or tradition it <example: our customary dinner celebration>

debt /det/ noun: money that is owed to someone else <example: He is in debt due to excessive spending.>

decade /'de-kād/ noun: a period of ten years <example: The 1990s were a decade of great change.>

distributor /də-'strə-byü-tər/ noun: a person or company that supplies goods to retailers <example: The distributor is responsible for getting the product to the customers.>

dramatic /drə-'ma-tik/ adjective: relating to or involving an exciting or dramatic event or situation <example: The sudden change in the weather was dramatic.>

endeavor /en-də-'vȯr/ noun: an attempt or effort to achieve a goal <example: It was a difficult

endeavor, but they were determined to succeed.>

entrepreneur /ˌän-trə-prə-ˈnər/ noun: a person who starts and runs a business <example: She is an entrepreneur who started her own company.>

fascinate /ˈfas-ə-ˌnāt/ verb: to interest or captivate someone greatly <example: The story of his life fascinated me.>

feature /ˈfē-chər/ noun: an aspect or quality that makes something notable or attractive <example: One of the features of the city is its beautiful parks.>

groundbreaking /'ground-'brā-kiNG/ adjective: involving new and innovative ideas or methods <example: groundbreaking technology.>

illustrate /'i-lə-strāt/ verb: to show or demonstrate something using examples or diagrams <example: The teacher illustrated the concept with a diagram.>

innovative /i-'nä-və-tiv/ adjective: introducing new ideas or methods <example: The company is known for its innovative products.>

investor /in-'ves-tər/ noun: a person or entity that invests money in a venture with the expectation of making a profit <example: He is a successful investor who invests in real estate.>

legacy /'le-gə-sē/ noun: something that is handed down from an ancestor or predecessor <example: The company's legacy is a commitment to quality and customer satisfaction.>

negotiate /nə-'gō-shē-āt/ verb: to discuss and reach an agreement with someone <example: They negotiated a deal to buy the company.>

overwhelming /ˌō-vər-'hwel-miNG/ adjective: too great or intense for someone to handle or cope with <example: The amount of work was

overwhelming, and he couldn't keep up.>

patriotic /pə-'trī-ə-tik/ adjective: relating to love for and devotion to one's country <example: He is a patriotic person who always supports his country.>

perseverance /ˌpər-sə-'vir-əns/ noun: the quality of continuing to try to do something even when it is difficult <example: She demonstrated great perseverance in the face of adversity.>

pompous /'päm-pəs/ adjective: having or showing an exaggerated sense of one's own importance <example: He is a pompous person

who thinks he is better than everyone else.>

prestigious /pre-'sti-jə-wəs/ adjective: respected and admired because of achievement, reputation, or social status <example: The university is one of the most prestigious in the country.>

propaganda /prə-'pä-gən-də/ noun: information, ideas, or opinions that are spread to promote a particular cause or ideology <example: The government used propaganda to convince people to support the war.>

replica /ˈre-plə-kə/ noun: an exact copy or reproduction of something <example: The museum has a replica of the ancient statue.>

salary /ˈsal-ə-rē/ noun: a fixed amount of money paid to an employee, typically on a monthly or annual basis <example: He negotiated a higher salary before accepting the job.>

testament /ˈte-stə-mənt/ noun: a statement or declaration that expresses one's beliefs or values <example: His life was a testament to his love of family and community.>

trajectory /trə-ˈjek-tə-rē/ noun: the path that an object or projectile follows through space <example: The trajectory of the rocket was carefully calculated.>

versatility /vər-sə-'tī-lə-tē/ noun: the ability to adapt or work with many different things or in various ways <example: She is known for her versatility in playing different musical instruments.>

SELECTED REFERENCES

Barrier, J. Michael (2007). The Animated Man: A Life of Walt Disney. Oakland, CA: University of California Press.

Canemaker, John (2001). Walt Disney's Nine Old Men and the Art of Animation. Burbank, CA: Disney Editions.

Eliot, Marc (1995). Walt Disney: Hollywood's Dark Prince. London: André Deutsch.

Krasniewicz, Louise (2010). Walt Disney: A Biography. Santa Barbara, CA: Greenwood Publishing.

Langer, Mark (2000). "Disney, Walt". American National Biography. Retrieved April 11, 2016.

Mannheim, Steve (2016). Walt Disney and the Quest for Community. Abingdon, Oxon: Routledge.

Mosley, Leonard (1990). Disney's World. Lanham, MD: Scarborough House.

Schickel, Richard (1986). The Disney Version: The Life, Times, Art and Commerce of Walt Disney. London: Pavilion Books.

Telotte, Jay P. (June 2, 2008). The Mouse Machine: Disney and Technology. Urbana, IL: University of Illinois Press.

Watts, Steven (2013). The Magic Kingdom: Walt Disney and the American Way of Life. Columbia, MO: University of Missouri Press.

Williams, Pat; Denney, James; Denney, Jim (2004). How to Be Like Walt: Capturing the Disney Magic Every Day of Your Life. Deerfield Beach, FL: Health Communications.

LETTER FROM THE AUTHOR

Dear Readers,

I hope you enjoyed this book and learned some take away that may help you as you continue to grow and make choices in life. Legends and icons can teach us about what we want to do and what we might not want to do. They can help us learn about ourselves and what decisions help and hurt people as they follow their dreams.

If you enjoyed learning about this icon, you could read about more in our Biographies for Kids series! Check out a free preview of another great biography at the back of this book.

Happy learning and may your dreams come true!

All the best,
Adam Kent

COLLECT THE WHOLE *GET SMART* BOOK SERIES

Here are just a few:

ROCKET
BOOKS

Join our book club for free book offers. For more info email:

info@rocketkidsbookclub.com

Made in the USA
Columbia, SC
16 October 2023

24525195R00065